A MIND FOR NUMBERS

at any age:

15 WAYS
TO EXERCISE YOUR BRAIN
TO THINK LIKE A SCIENTIST

Winston J. Duncan

© Copyright 2015 by Winston J. Duncan - All rights reserved.

This document is geared towards providing exact and reliable information in regards to the topic and issue covered. The publication is sold with the idea that the publisher is not required to render accounting, officially permitted, or otherwise, qualified services. If advice is necessary, legal or professional, a practiced individual in the profession should be ordered.

- From a Declaration of Principles which was accepted and approved equally by a Committee of the American Bar Association and a Committee of Publishers and Associations.

In no way is it legal to reproduce, duplicate, or transmit any part of this document in either electronic means or in printed format. Recording of this publication is strictly prohibited and any storage of this document is not allowed unless with written permission from the publisher. All rights reserved.

The information provided herein is stated to be truthful and consistent, in that any liability, in terms of inattention or otherwise, by any usage or abuse of any policies, processes, or directions contained within is the solitary and utter responsibility of the recipient reader. Under no circumstances will any legal responsibility or blame be held against the publisher for any reparation, damages, or monetary loss due to the information herein, either directly or indirectly.

Respective authors own all copyrights not held by the publisher.

The information herein is offered for informational purposes solely, and is universal as so. The presentation of the information is without contract or any type of guarantee assurance.

The trademarks that are used are without any consent, and the publication of the trademark is without permission or backing by the trademark owner. All trademarks and brands within this book are for clarifying purposes only and are the owned by the owners themselves, not affiliated with this document.

Table of Contents

INTRODUCTION	1
CHAPTER ONE: EVOLUTION OF THINKING	3
CHAPTER TWO: HOW WE EXERCISE OUR BRAINS LIKE SCIENTISTS ON A DAILY BASIS	6
Observing	6
Inferring	7
Predictions	8
Classifying Data	8
Models	9
Communication	9
CHAPTER THREE: UNDERSTANDING THE NEED TO EXERCISE THE BRAIN	11
CHAPTER FOUR: CREATING A PROCESS	15
CHAPTER FIVE: LEARN TO OBSERVE	19
CHAPTER SIX: INFER AND INTERPRET WITH AN EDUCATED GUESS	22
CHAPTER SEVEN: PRACTICE, AND THEN PRACTICE SOME MORE	24
CHAPTER EIGHT: MAKE PREDICTIONS THAT KEEP YOU FOCUSED	27
CHAPTER NINE: IT'S ALL IN THE DETAILS	29
CHAPTER TEN: UNRAVEL THE CONTRADICTIONS	31
Opening Up the Possibilities in the Mind	31

    Suspending Judgment — *32*

    Cast a Wide Net for New Ideas — *33*

CHAPTER ELEVEN: BE SKEPTICAL — 34

CHAPTER TWELVE: AVOID THINKING PITFALLS — 37

    Confirmation Bias — *39*

    Attribution Bias — *39*

    Agreement Bias — *40*

    In-group Bias — *41*

    Gambler's Fallacy — *41*

    Post-Purchase Rationalization — *42*

    Neglecting Probability — *43*

    Observational Selection Bias — *44*

    Status-Quo Bias — *45*

    Negativity Bias — *45*

    Bandwagon Effect — *46*

    Projection Bias — *47*

    The Current Moment Bias — *47*

    Anchoring Effect — *48*

    Hindsight Bias — *48*

CHAPTER THIRTEEN: SEEING THROUGH SCIENTIFIC EYES EACH DAY — 50

    The Crossword Puzzle — *50*

    Using a Recipe to Cook a Meal — *51*

    Handling Repairs — *51*

CHAPTER FOURTEEN: HOW TO OVERCOME BIASES — 53

    Recognizing the Bias   53

    Note the Three Reasons You Have a Bias   53

    Strange   53

    Betrayal   53

    Attractiveness   54

    Ask Questions   54

    Face It   54

    Take It One Step at a Time   55

CHAPTER FIFTEEN: USE MODELS AND STATISTICS WISELY   56

CHAPTER SIXTEEN: THINK LIKE A MATHEMATICIAN   60

    Question Everything   60

    Write in Sentences   61

    Use Converse Statements   61

    Use Contrapositives   62

    Consider Extreme Examples   62

    Create Your Own Examples   62

    Where are Assumptions Used   62

    Start with the Complicated   63

    Ask What If   63

    Communicate   63

CONCLUSION   65

INTRODUCTION

Scientists have long been revered for their intelligence, problem solving skills and intense knowledge. Rather than being personality traits of an individual, these attributes are actually well developed skills. This is excellent news for the average person, because it means that with practice, one can train their brain to think like a scientist.

Scientific thinking is methodical. One step follows another, and from following guided steps, one is always likely to achieve a result. This type of thinking is focused on problem solving. This involves fully understanding all the variables for a particular problem, and then analyzing these variables one at a time until a solution surfaces.

Scientists are masters of strategic thinking. In essence, strategic thinking is also methodical as it has a planning process, and added on to this is innovation, strategic planning and operational planning. Using strategies helps the scientist achieve greater success in their endeavors. They are persistent, never giving up until they finally get the desired result, and viewing every failure as an opportunity. When calculating mathematical problems, this is valuable, as when these problems increase in complexity, achieving a result becomes more difficult. The brain that is geared towards scientific thinking will never give up.

There are ten ways in which you can train your brain to think like a scientist and these are outlined as: -

1. Creating a process
2. Learn to observe
3. Infer and interpret with an educated guess

4. Practice, and the practice some more

5. Make predictions that keep you focused

6. It's all in the details

7. Unravel the contradictions

8. Be skeptical

9. Avoid thinking pitfalls

10. Seeing through scientific eyes each day

This book is designed to help you master each of these ways, thereby equipping you with excellent skills. With sufficient and consistent practice, the methods and tools that you get from this book will improve your brain activity and sharpen your focus, helping you think like a scientist.

CHAPTER ONE:
EVOLUTION OF THINKING

Before you fully dive into this book about how to think like a scientist, let's first take a look at the evolution of thinking. It'll help you understand your thinking process, as well as understand what it means to think like a scientist. We'll start with two billion years ago, when we looked nothing remotely close to a human, but were a single-celled organism.

It took us until just two million years ago for us to leave the trees for caves, and only two hundred thousand years ago until we became what are known as modern man. When language arrived is still a mystery, but an educated guess puts it as around fifty-thousand years ago. After that, it becomes a lot easier to track.

With Aristotle, around 2,500 years ago, formal logic showed up in our history. Around 400 years ago is when Francis Bacon developed the scientific method. Not long after the scientific method was invented, the Royal Society of London for Improving Natural Knowledge was created. The thinking behind these two milestones in our history was that we now knew how to define what good science was and had an organization that would monitor how science was being conducted.

The first time we used the scientific method in 1025 AD was in the 18th century when a physician known as James Lind discovered the curative properties of oranges and lemons. His discovery came about because he had used the scientific method to separate people into several groups that were randomized. He figured out that the oranges and lemons helped when treating sailors who had scurvy. He didn't have a name for the substance in the oranges and lemons that helped, but we would later call it vitamin C.

The idea of statistical thinking is still just a baby at just a little over a hundred years old. Ronald Fisher, a British statistician, brought about the use of the p-value to propose limits of chance versus significance.

The point of all this is to illustrate that we have only been thinking logically for the last 2,500 years, and we've only been able to use the scientific method for the past 400 years. In the meantime, we had to use other methods of thinking in order to survive, so what were they?

When we were living in tribes, the best thing we could do to survive was to emulate others. If our tribe mate was never ill, we would follow him or her around and mimic their every move so that we didn't become ill, too. For millions of years we honed this practice of observing a positive trait, mimicking the behaviors of those who had the traits, and repeating.

Yet we've only had 0.0002% of that time to hone our skills for logical thinking. That means when we think logically, we have to go against those millions of years of hardwired thinking of copycats. We have to fight against the very evolution that kept us alive and go out of our way to think logically and scientifically.

Since the invention of the MRI, we've been studying our brains. Neuroscientists have been wondering about the impact of independent thinking on our brains and its activity, and they've discovered some interesting tidbits of information. One of those tidbits is very provocative and interesting. Those who think logically were studied under an MRI machine while they were thinking in this manner, and the neuroscientists found that there is an actual pain of independence. The amygdalae of those who think logically were lit up and the brain was producing stress signals. Thinking logically is actually emotionally stressful; however, it's a necessary occurrence for those who want to think like a scientist.

Therefore, we're not genetically equipped to think in a logical or scientific manner because it's an evolutionary development that's still in its infancy. Many logical thinkers become frustrated that there isn't more scientific research and data in the news media; however, can we really become upset with a species that has survived doing what they're currently doing? That doesn't make mimicry correct, but it's like punishing a tree for oozing sap when its limb is cut off.

So what can you do about it?

Correcting everyone's behavior is simply not feasible and it's not necessarily the right path to choose, but you have already shown an interest in changing your path in life. You've picked up this book on logical thinking and you have a desire to learn, and this is the most paramount ingredient to success. The next ingredient is to find a mentor, and I'm hoping that I can be your first mentor with this book, but you should find another in your field of study that you can speak with in person.

CHAPTER TWO:
HOW WE EXERCISE OUR BRAINS LIKE SCIENTISTS ON A DAILY BASIS

Did you know that we all think on a scientific basis every day? That's right, every decision you make and every though process you have about those decisions is a scientific process. I know you might not believe me, so let's take a look at some examples. This will help you think more like a scientist throughout your daily activities so that you can practice.

Observing

We have five senses that we currently know of: sight, sound, touch, taste, and hearing. When we use one or more of these senses to determine or gather information, we're making an observation. For example, you might determine that something is sharp because you poked your finger with it, or that an object is green because you're looking at it. Scientists use their five senses to determine whether things are dangerous, what their texture, shape, color, smell, and sometimes even taste are. Of course, there are some senses it would be best not to test out because some things might be poisonous, like gasoline, so they don't always use all five senses.

Scientists also use instruments in order to make their observations more thorough, such as using a microscope to determine the width or length of a hair, or a centrifuge to separate blood particles.

What matters about observation is that you can record these tidbits of information as facts and not as a guess. You know that a blade of grass is green or that the knife is sharp. You can put that information down as a fact so that you can use it later in order to help solve a problem. If you cannot say for sure the information you're gathering is a fact, then you must put it under a separate category and try to prove or disprove whether it's true.

Inferring

Once you've observed something happening or used one of your senses to determine that an object is a specific color, for example, then you need to interpret that data and make an educated guess, also known as an inference. Inferences are an interpretation that you've made of the data you've gathered, but they don't always mean you're correct. This is where most people stop when they make an assumption, but a scientist knows that they need to dig deeper.

As an example, perhaps you hear a rooster crowing before you open your eyes. From your childhood, you've learned a rooster crows in the morning, most of the time. So you make the assumption that the rooster is crowing because it's currently morning; however, you might be wrong. The rooster could be crowing because he is hurt or there is someone disturbing his sleep. Therefore, you've inferred that it's morning, but you don't really know unless you dive into the information further.

Another example might be that you hear the sound of a cat purring. You automatically assume the cat is happy, but did you know that cats will purr if they're injured or upset? Therefore, without *seeing* the cat and observing how it reacts with someone else, you don't know for sure the cat is happy.

Scientists understand that these educated guesses are valid, but they're not solid and thought out. Therefore, they need more information.

Predictions

Most of us watch a prediction on a daily basis. It's known as weather predictions. Predictions are inferences that have been made due to past events and currently evidence that matches up with those past events. We have fancy computer models to teach us all about the weather, but meteorologists are taught how to predict the weather manually so that they understand how the entire process works.

Let's use a more real-life example. Do you remember when you were a child and you stepped into the rain for the first time? Perhaps it was a cool fall rain, or maybe it was a warm, summer rain. If we see rain outside and it's autumn, we will predict that it's going to be cool rain because it was cool before when we experienced it; however, we don't really know until we step out into the rain. That's a prediction based upon past experiences and current data.

Classifying Data

Classifying data is simply grouping it together so that you can see how it relates to one another. For example, a scientist is studying three different plants. One plant has a yellow flower, the other a blue, and the final a red. He would group that information together under one category known as 'Color.' He may then take measurements of the plants leaves, and classify that data under 'Leaf Measurements.'

You might practice classification of data on a daily basis. Perhaps you are searching for information in an old yearbook and you want to find someone's picture. You first look at the grade they were in, and then you search for them by the first letter of their last name, alphabetically. This is an example of data that has been organized and classified.

Models

Do you remember playing with those tiny army men or those baby dolls when you were a child? While they were rudimentary in the fact that they might not have been to scale or they didn't have great detail, they were models. When you made a mud-pie that was smaller than a real pie, you were making a model. When you look at something on the computer screen that's a drawing of an object that will be much larger, that's a model. Even when you draw something on notebook paper, such as a tree, it's a model.

Some models can be to scale while others don't really need to be to scale. Models are great for understanding something that's very complex, such as the reproductive system or the inside of a cell in science class. The best example of a model is a solar system model that shows how the planets rotate around the sun and what color they are.

A scientist uses a model in order to simplify a complicated idea or information. They're usually generated by computers, but we used to draw models by hand on pieces of paper, and even make them with wooden sculptures when we didn't have paper.

Communication

On a daily basis you talk with your friends and family, and you listen to what others are saying, and you even write messages via e-mail, texting, or some still use snail-mail. Communication is something that every human being does, and it doesn't even have to be with other people. Sometimes we communicate with ourselves and we communicate with a pet, such as a dog we want to sit down or roll over. In order to communicate effectively, we must do more than just speak, we must also listen.

Scientists understand that we have to listen on a daily basis in order to gather, share, and form opinions about information. Then we share that information, data, results, and opinions with others in order to get *their* opinions. Scientists will use a formal method of communicating like the Internet, reports, and meetings, but they may also have informal communication between each other in the field.

As you can see, we all think like a scientist on a daily basis, at least up to the part where we observe, but a true scientist moves beyond that point. They make educated guess and then explore those guesses and turn them into truths or untruths. Then they explore further to discover more truths about their surroundings. They're always learning.

CHAPTER THREE:
UNDERSTANDING THE NEED TO EXERCISE THE BRAIN

The brain controls all of our thinking, and is constantly sending messages throughout our body guiding our actions. Just like you would go to the gym to build up a muscle and improve your strength, you also need to continuously work on developing your brain to bring the most out from it.

Scientists have mastered the art of keeping their brains active, focused and in constant development. They somehow seem to increase their knowledge and reasoning over time, where most people experience diminished brain activity and capacity. When working with numbers, it is particularly important to have a brain that is 'switched on', to ensure you can get accurate results, as well as to avoid the mental taxation that can result from working out problems.

For this reason, understanding brain plasticity is key. Brain plasticity is the brains natural ability to remodel itself throughout life.

The brain is made up of one hundred billion neurons, and early on, scientists believed the ability to create new neurons ceased after birth. However, they now understand that the brain is able to reorganize itself and create fresh connections, or even create new neurons.

Think about someone who has just had a stroke. If the scientists were accurate, someone who had suffered a stroke and lost the ability to speak would not be able to regain that ability. There are many stroke victims out there who would disprove this theory that neurons are static and never-changing. Their brains were able to rewire themselves in order to allow the person to speak again.

Brain plasticity is dynamic, meaning that it's ever-changing. While for some this might be encouraging information, for others you might be thinking, but doesn't that mean it can falter at any time? Your brain's plasticity varies by your age and some changes are predominant when you're an infant, a child, and a teenager. It also involves more than just neurons. Your brain's plasticity includes other cells such as the glial and vascular cells. So their health is just as important in your brain's ability to easily rewire itself.

Another interesting fact about your brain's plasticity is that it can happen for two reasons: learning and experiences, as well as memory formation, and brain damage. The way your brain changes is not always for the better, so be aware of how you're treating it and taking care of it. Some of you might be thinking that now you know your brain is basically able to heal itself, you can abuse it. Remember that when you damage your brain, it takes a longer time to heal when you're an adult. While you still have neurons, they're not as agile as they once were.

So how does your brain keep up with everything that you learn and still retain the ability to change when you're an adult? It's a lot like trimming the dead leaves off a plant. Your brain periodically goes through all of your neurons, and the ones that have not been used the longest are the ones that are culled.

There are two different types of brain plasticity. There's functional plasticity which allows the brain to move neural pathways from a damaged part of the brain to an undamaged part of the brain. This is the type of plasticity that's in action when a person is in a car accident or has a stroke and suffers brain damage. Then there's structural plasticity, which is what we'll be focusing on in this book.

Structural plasticity is the brain's ability to restructure itself in order for you to learn. When you learn something new, your brain creates a neural pathway so that you are able to retain that information. That's the plasticity that you really want to exercise, so that you can learn easily and be fluid in your learning.

The brain is not static; it is always taking in new information, as well as releasing information. The brain is continuously taught how to pay attention, increase its functioning speed, retain memories, navigate problems, develop social or people skills and build on intelligence. In order to exercise your brain to think like a scientist, you need to be able to control and improve your basic sensory skills.

Over time, the brain begins to lose efficiency in certain roles – that is if you have not taught your brain otherwise. Some of the things that scientists have mastered include:

- Speed – They are able to think of their feet. Without exercising the brain, activities around you remain at the same pace, but your ability to process these activities will slow down.

- Brightness – Scientists have sharp minds, always ready to process information effectively. A mind that does not engage in this type of thinking starts to get tired, and also acts tired. Dealing with issues then takes longer and can be a taxing process.

- Accuracy – Scientists pay attention to detail. By doing so, they ensure that they have covered all the bases necessary to solve a problem.

- Clarity – When addressing any issue, 'noise' or 'disruption' from the outside world is inevitable. This noise can easily lead one away from the intended path. Scientists are able to discern these noises, and focus on the main problem. This means that the solution is clear and well represented, without unnecessary variables.

- Recognition – Understanding information more deeply comes naturally to scientists. They are able to look for detail, and identify relevant information.

- Recording – As scientists become more mature in their professions, they are able to control their ability to learn, and rise to the occasion. Their minds become better with age, rather than diminishing in capacity.

When working with numbers, these roles that the brain takes on are particularly important. Numbers report information, and this information is often used to draw conclusions.

CHAPTER FOUR:
CREATING A PROCESS

All mathematical calculation follows a pre-designed process. While in school, one had to memorize formulas or understand the 'method' in order to solve mathematical problems. Each step in a method was important, and if you arrived at a correct answer, without being able to explain how you got there, it was possible that your teacher would mark your answer wrong.

Your brain is also process oriented, piecing together certain steps to fulfill a purpose. For example, following a good night's sleep, you want to brush your teeth immediately after you wake up. Your brain is trained to get you to open your eyes, get out of bed, walk towards the bathroom, put toothpaste on the brush and then brush your teeth, thereby following a process. Although it may seem simple and obvious, it is not. This is only realized once a step in the process is skipped or unattainable.

Scientific thinking entails you asking certain questions when following a process. These are the '5 W's' – who, what, when, where and why. These 5 W's are excellent when solving problems, as they attempt to exhaustively offer insight on the problem. Brainstorming entails evaluating the existing situation and discussing various solutions, following which, one is chosen. The positives and negatives are then analyzed, and thereafter an informed decision is made. With practice, the brain can be trained to evaluate situations by weighing the positives and negatives, as well as considering what alternatives exist before making a final decision.

Within the steps of the process, ensure that you always ask questions. This helps you go through each step exhaustively. The questions that could be asked include, how do I address this situation? Is there any data I have missed? Are there new ideas I can explore? Am I fully aware of all the variables? Can I build on my results? These questions differ from the 5 w's, and have more to do with state of mind. They are especially applicable when dealing with mathematical issues. To think like a scientist, question everything, as answering the questions helps you to cover all your bases.

A simple process that can exercise the brain is as follows.

- Start with writing out the problem that you are addressing as a question.

- Brainstorm with like-minded individuals to get an idea of what information you will need to help you answer the question.

- Create a plan that will help you develop or identify the information you need.

- Clearly define all factors that you will refer to, and the protocol that shall be followed for collecting the information.

- Gather the information that you need and ensure that it is from a trustworthy source as you do so. Make sure you have enough to fill in any data collection gaps that may arise.

- As you go along, you may find that you have to modify your definitions and protocols. Be open minded and allow yourself to utilize all new information.

- Present your work in a visual manner, with a chart, mind map or illustrations. It is easier to assimilate information through diagrams than it is in written text.

A normal process would usually be concluded at this point, however, a scientific process requires several more steps. Extending the questions that the brain will ask is essential to exercising the brain, and is something that scientist have perfected. The additional steps include:

- Returning to your original questions. Review your results and consider whether you have actually been effective in finding an answer. If you have not found an answer, you can then continue to analyses the data from different perspectives until you do.

- At this point, even though you may have found an answer, ask another question which is, so what? This all important additional question will help you to explore further possibilities, and reevaluate your results. Scientists cover all their bases when addressing issues. Your brain can be trained to do more than accept what is at face value. Your brain can be taught to look for variations and further analyses what appears to be a complete answer. This will be support the initial problem, by offering deeper insight and exploring novel ideas for improvement of the results.

- Evaluate your results and identify anything else the data reveals.

- Now, where do you go from here? You can decide to continue with your exploration or to accept your results.

- In any case, you need to decide what the next important steps you want to take are.

These steps reveal that for scientific thinking, you should be able to constantly push your brain. The end of a process does not necessarily mean the end of an exploration. It simply presents an opportunity to change your point of view and continue thinking.

CHAPTER FIVE:
LEARN TO OBSERVE

Observation directly relates to your consciousness and perspectives. To be able to observe, you must have the ability to look at things from another's point of view or put yourself in another's shoes. This ensures that you have an unbiased view of any situation. Observation entails viewing every aspect of your environment, and then using this information to address an issue. Observation is more than simply seeing people, situations or things and drawing conclusions. It actually entails using all five senses to get information.

The five senses are sight, sound, smell, taste and touch. They can be used all at once, or individually based on the situation being assessed. Scientists have found ways in which they can enhance these senses so that they are able to understand a problem more deeply. When exercising the brain, increasing sharpness begins with the senses. As your brain improves the clarity with which it registers information from all your sensory organs, you improve your responses and ability to store information. Scientists have developed tools that further help them to enhance their senses and review information. For example, in order to see an object more clearly, a scientist will use a microscope. This brings to life parts of the object by allowing for a more detailed view, thereby improving the scientist's sense of sight. Other non-physical tools can be developed. Take for example sound. When having a conversation, we hear each other's voices as we exchange information and possibly some background noise like birds chirping or vehicles moving. One can then draw a basic conclusion as to the location of the conversation, whether those conversing were male or female, and even their approximated age.

A scientist will observe things more deeply. To think like a scientist, you cannot take any aspect of the conversation for granted. A scientist would listen to all the background noises, and may be able to provide additional details such as whether there was anyone else in the room. They are attuned to paying attention to detail, and amplifying those details to explore additional solutions.

As the brain registers this information from our sensory organs more clearly, we are then better able to respond to the information and store it. The ability of the brain to retain information is worth highlighting here. When working with numbers, one must remember methodologies and formulas so as to work out a problem. Having highly attuned sensory organs makes it easier to remember all aspects necessary to address the problem. Without all these in mind, it may prove impossible to resolve a mathematical issue.

When evaluating a mathematical problem for example, how can you use observation to your advantage? You can teach your brain to register details, looking beyond the surface problem to deeper understand how the numbers work. Missing details is the main cause of errors and confusion which then limits both your results and your thinking. In fact, brains that miss details often have been found to slow down, basically so that the brain can avoid making further mistakes.

When observing, results must be reported accurately and factually. Our brains have ways that they interpret information, and when we report results, they are usually peppered with our own opinions, understanding and internal references. To think like a scientist, you must be objective, and avoid bias.

Once you begin to actively observe, you will find that you are inundated with information that features many details. If you want to think like a scientist, you must learn how to pay attention to the details which matter, and refuse to focus on the details that do not matter. This is particularly important when working with numbers, so as to save you time and other resources, and also, so as to ensure that you do not use the wrong information when trying to work out a solution.

When observing, you must also be sure of the source of your information. Scientists have a keen sense when it comes to verification of their sources, as in many cases they are dealing with sensitive information.

Do not underestimate the power of the subconscious mind. Scientists operate at a high level of consciousness about the world around them. As they take in information, they are able to refer to it in the future, even though they may not have the need to use all the information they have at the present moment. With the passage of time, their subconscious mind, and level of consciousness increase in order to process more information. Scientists are able to assimilate information more deeply than the regular person, because they consciously tap into their subconscious mind to explore scenarios. When one walks into a room, you might observe the furniture, paintings and wall color. If you have succeeded in exercising your brain, you will also remember the finer details like the items on tables, temperature of the room and whether the window was open or not.

CHAPTER SIX:
INFER AND INTERPRET WITH AN EDUCATED GUESS

Scientists are curious about how things work. One of the ways that they are able discover so much about things is their curiosity to understand the world around them. To satisfy their curiosity, they ask questions that intend to discover detailed information, rather than just understand the surface cause of an issue. They try to understand different phenomena, methodologies, systems and models by breaking them down into variables and assessing each variable. They are able to turn the bigger picture, into several smaller pictures. Scientists look for possible reasons and explanations to the phenomena that they are investigating. This is most easily done by developing a hypothesis. A hypothesis is a statement which, when answered, will prove or disprove a condition under investigation.

When creating and evaluating a hypothesis, a scientist ensures that they do so from a factual point of view, not an emotional or opinionated one. Every person has biases. To be able to think like a scientist, you must be able to identify and confront your personal biases. Without this, it is highly likely that you will taint your results, and they will not be reliable. Teach yourself how to take you out of the equation whenever you are addressing a problem, and it will be easier to follow existing guidelines, formulas or methods of working out the issue.

Once you have defined your hypothesis, you can achieve results by testing it. A scientist would first create a control test, which is one where the variables do not change. The scientist then attempts to get results by applying different variables and observing the results.

When working with numbers, this system of achieving results is thorough, as you are able to review all the alternatives. Scientists use three methods when making an educated guess, and these are, inductive, deductive and causal reasoning. To exercise your brain, when presented with a problem, look at it from as many angles as possible. For example, you could assess what caused the problem, investigate the problem and identify the reasons that may arise, or what the solution to the problem is, working backwards to understand how the problem arose, or whether the problem is created by an internal or external force.

Once you have gone through making your educated guess, an investigation can be conducted and data analyzed. From the information generated, you will then be ready to draw a solid conclusion and share your results. Your solid conclusion will be as a result of your brain working with facts, and being able to assess those facts from various points of view, thereby eliminated unnecessary information or inconclusive scenarios. Factual thinking is also more reliable, as it is easier to rationalize and explain your point of view.

In addition to being factual, a scientist also uses their imagination to idealize methods to attain their results. Imagination increases the realm of possibility, and opens up the mind to finding different ways to address any issue. By tapping into your imagination, you can unleash your creativity thereby allowing your brain to assimilate information and identify the bigger picture. Looking at the bigger picture allows your brain to open itself up to endless problem solving possibilities.

CHAPTER SEVEN:
PRACTICE, AND THEN PRACTICE SOME MORE

Scientists experiment. Experimenting means that they try and try and try to solve a particular problem in as many ways as possible until they get a result. Giving up is not an option. Emotions are processed in the brain, and guide human behavior. In a situation where someone is working on an experiment or problem, and they are unable to find the solution, frustration is usually the result. Following which, the individual may simply give up because it is too difficult to find a solution. Scientists have developed the skill of taking each mistake or failure as an opportunity to search deeper for another answer. The mistake is simply a variable that is eliminated, and another course of action is taken.

To teach your brain not to 'shut down' or 'give up' when facing a problem, you must develop the scientific skill of practice, practice and then practice some more. When something is not right, therein lies the opportunity to keep working on it until it comes together. You must eliminate from your mind the word failure, and look at each instance where you do not attain a result as an opportunity. Failure is a prerequisite of success and a learning process that brings you close to your ultimate goal. Sometimes failure does not come about because of getting the wrong result, but because of a lack of persistence.

Since there is every possibility that a scientist will not achieve the result being searched for during an experiment, the scientist has to be open to receiving alternative suggestions from peers or colleagues, to expand their view and see the bigger picture. A scientist is able to choose a situation that will change his perspective. This will help in the development of more theories. Our brains are geared towards being right, and believing in our own achievements. That is why it is often difficult for us to ask for help, or even to admit when we are wrong and graciously accept correction. To think like a scientist, we need to reevaluate how we react to situations where someone is giving us correction. If your reaction is anger or displeasure, when it happens, stop. Listen to the correction, and separate fact from emotion. The brain can be trained to listen and assimilate information, rather than to listen and react. However, it will entail a conscious effort on your part to track your emotions, and change your reactions.

A busy brain is a productive brain. Ensure that your brain is being challenged with various scenarios and solution approaches. Scientists work tirelessly to produce results, and will continue to tackle a problem until they do so. If you are not familiar with continued practice, it may seem very challenging to keep your mind constantly busy. What you could do to get yourself to that point, would be to keep a detailed journal of everything you are dealing with. The journal should include details on daily observations, as well as how far you have moved forward, what your future plans are and anything else that is relevant to resolving your issue. It is important to maintain this every day for optimal results.

To stimulate the brain, you need to read constantly, and like scientists, this will create a skill that keeps your brain active. Not only is reading excellent for improving brain function, it is also great for gathering information.

Writing things down is a sure method to 'wake up' for the brain. When you write things down, you are able to work through a problem step by step, until you have written down the solution. Your brain can process information faster and with more accuracy when things are written down.

An important part of practice and thinking like a scientist involves rest. Once you have stimulated your brain, and are constantly thinking about different methodologies to address an issue, you must take a break and rest. Like any muscle in the body, a brain can get stressed leading to headaches or migraines or other health issues. The brain also requires time to rejuvenate itself in order to be continuously productive. Once you rest your brain, you are able to focus more clearly. Your brain is then able to connect unrelated factors in new ways. Some simple ways of resting the brain include taking a walk, looking out at the sun, meditation, exercise or sitting calmly with no distractions.

Finally, scientists are passionate about what they are doing and this passion drives them to think differently and deeper than the ordinary person. When training your brain to think like a scientist, you must have the innate passion to find out information. This makes it easier for your brain to process information, as you become naturally receptive. Scientists enjoy what they do, and once they have made a breakthrough, they celebrate. So in addition to working hard, focusing, continuous practice, keeping your brain busy and resting, enjoyment and celebration is also essential to stimulate the brain.

CHAPTER EIGHT:
MAKE PREDICTIONS THAT KEEP YOU FOCUSED

Predicting a future occurrence is important when attempting to understand the occurrence, as well as the steps that are necessary to lead up to it. Scientists predict future occurrences, in order to change the circumstances around these occurrences, leading to a better result.

The way they do it is by using observations which give first-hand information, and leaning on their existing knowledge. They base their predictions on current evidence as well as previous experiences. The brain can learn how to make predictions, by understand that past behavior is a good predictor of future behavior.

If a variable behaves a certain way several times in one situation, it will continue to do so. Unless some changes are made to the process, the results are likely to be the same. Making predictions creates awareness, and helps the brain develop alternatives to issues that may be addressed.

An easy way that this can be done is mentally classifying variables so that they are easier to address. Scientists create numerous classifications when addressing problems, such as dividing their population based on similarities like age, size, color, purpose and so on. This makes it easier to understand how individuals or items connect or relate to each other.

From this, scientists are able to create models which help them to understand complex situations in simple ways. Instructions on steps to be taken can be given, and when followed, these can lead to a specific result. It is easy to teach your brain how to do this. For example, you want to assemble a DIY cupboard that you have bought. You open the box, and using the instructions, are able to put together all the pieces in a specified order so that the final result is a table.

Also, combining classifications and reviewing the effects is often done by scientists, as they seek to understand changes in the environment. When faced with a problem that has more than one variable, you can try to review what the answers would be based on combining and comparing the results.

Making connections between seemingly dissimilar concepts could bring about a breakthrough. When thinking like a scientist, you should consider what the bridge or connection could be between variables that are highly unlikely to go together.

When making a prediction, you can visualize your end result. As a problem solving tool, visualization is quite effective. Look at your dilemma as you would a picture, and where possible use diagrams to analyses it. Diagrams are easier to understand than text, especially if several pages of data can be illustrated on a single page diagram. Your brain will be able to view the diagram, and also try to understand what may be causing the issue. Visualization also makes it easier to see the whole picture, and consider the available options.

CHAPTER NINE:
IT'S ALL IN THE DETAILS

Scientists are masters of dissecting the details of a problem. That is why you can present them with three or four variables requesting for their insight and feedback, and receive pages worth of information on how those variables affect each other. It is important to them to look further than the surface, and to search deeply into the reasons that a certain phenomenon is occurring. To think like a scientist and develop an eye for detail, you can try using a control test.

When carrying out experiments, the control test is key as it becomes the main reference point for all the other tests. The control test is a test that has no variables. It is also known as the main test and is used as for comparison with all the other results. Take for example you are baking a batch of cookies, and want to evaluate how changes in ingredients will affect the final result. You would start with a standardized recipe, which would be your control test. To start, you would follow your standard recipe and take note of the results. These results could include cooking time, final look, texture, flavor and so on. Using the same standardized recipe that you started with, you add or take away ingredients to produce new batches, and you should become aware of how these changes affect the original recipe. By noting each change, you have an idea of how a variation in a detail can change the final output. As a scientist, it is essential that you keep track of any information you receive.

You can utilize the same principle when you are dealing with numbers. In fact, you will find that this is the methodology used in algebra or for basic problem solving. Once you are aware of a standard formula, the "control test" of your mathematical problem, you can then use the formula, adding variations as you go along to suit the conditions of the problem. For example, you may be working on payroll information, trying to evaluate how to justify increasing the salaries of certain employees. When everyone joins the organization at a certain level, they all receive the same salary. In order to justify the increases, you can give value to certain elements, for example always meeting targets, increasing revenue, diversifying portfolio, improving your education or qualifications and so on. It is these little details that need to be logically and strategically assessed, so that any increases in salary are not only backed by fact, but can easily be justified, evaluated and measured.

When scientists use this technique, they make sure to test as many variables as possible because by doing so, they are able to achieve a more thorough answer. It is possible to get your brain to work in a similar manner by considering all possible scenarios and their likely outcomes. Once you have done so, you can make an informed decision based on your available information.

CHAPTER TEN:
UNRAVEL THE CONTRADICTIONS

Just as no two people are the same, a mathematical problem may be solved using two different methodologies, yet the answers will be exactly the same. This often time has people believe that there is evidence of contradictions, or that they are dealing with a paradoxical situation. In fact, a heated debate on methodology and similar findings can make solving mathematical riddles both stressful and contentious.

When thinking like a scientist, this is the sort of situation that should peak your interest and in effect get your creative juices flowing. A situation which presents contradicting information allows for investigation that goes to the heart of the matter, where you follow logical steps and possibly use a check list to ensure that you have covered all of your bases. It also allows the scientists to think outside of the box, especially if a situation arises where one of the methodologies needs to be properly justified. Scientists are always interested in looking at two or more well established findings that appear to contradict each other for various reasons.

Opening Up the Possibilities in the Mind

1. The first reason is they need to think outside the box. Despite having extensive problem solving knowledge, and being equipped with rich skills to address a range of situations, scientist are still able to admit that they do not know it all. These contradictory situations present them with opportunities to delve into the unknown, increase their knowledge and find their way around a mystery or misunderstood criterion. By thinking outside the box, they ensure that their brains are always receptive to learning new ideas and improved methods

of thinking. They are willing to consider radical approaches to problem solving so that they can fully understand contradictory methodologies. When working with numbers this becomes vital. Maintaining a rigid stance in regards to how one can reach a result or reviewing alternative types of evaluations may negatively limit the problem solver, putting them at a disadvantage with others. The constantly changing and improving methodologies in mathematics needs people with brains that are more open minded and willing to accept change.

Suspending Judgment

2. The second reason is that unravelling contradictions helps to suspend judgments. A good scientist does not think of a problem as right or wrong, rather the approach could be why or why not. Judgment should not be made on the methodology or the outcome until everything has been done and it is the conclusion that is being reviewed or addressed. Evaluating contradictions helps the scientist assess deep conceptual and analytic foundations that are affecting the conflicting conclusions or methodologies. When these evaluations are done without any judgment, it helps the scientist review evidence through a new lens. For brain development, this is essential as it helps avoid developing habits in thinking and assessment. A habit is difficult to break, and greatly limits the thinkers ability to see beyond the habit. Once you have taught your brain to use a single set of criteria to assess a situation, it becomes a real challenge to even consider alternatives. Suspending judgment is akin to keeping an open mind at all time to allow for the consideration of a range of alternatives.

Cast a Wide Net for New Ideas

3. The third reason is so that you can cast a wide net for new ideas and supporting evidence. Reviewing contradictions should help your brain consider information that may have previously been nonsensical. This is because you are able to review more solutions that the potentially obvious. By casting a wide net, you may opt to review other fields, consider cross disciplinary research or attempt to try a few way of dealing with arising issues. When working with numbers, this strategy will make it easier for you to remain up to date with the latest findings on addressing issues. On top of that, your brain will be able to develop new ideas as it goes through unfamiliar information, and you should gain valuable insight that will allow new patterns of thinking to emerge.

Sometimes when you begin to unravel the contradictions, you may establish that these contradictions exist as they reside in different disciplines. Mathematically, this can help you understand why methodologies may be different for the same issue. Take for example the calculation of IRR (Internal Rate of Return). It is used in financial management for the time value of money, as well as in project management to ascertain the validity of the project. In both disciplines, the answers may be the same, although the methodology used and the explanation for the steps used may be as different as night and day. However, you can teach your brain to understand the differences in the methodologies so that they can be used where appropriate. This trains the brain to explore areas outside of what is expected, to enable the unravelling of the contradictions.

CHAPTER ELEVEN: BE SKEPTICAL

According to Nobel Prize winning physicist Richard Feynman, "You must not fool yourself as you are the easiest person to fool." This statement is highly significant when referring to the workings of your brain. The human brain can be "arrogant". Often when we know a little, we believe we know a lot. The issue with this is that we then begin to limit our ability to assimilate new information, because after all, if we know so much what more is there for us to learn. This causes us to create behaviors and thinking patterns that revolve around just what we know, creating a situation where we become set in our ways for taking action. Once we master a particular way of doing things, we may practice it until we get it perfect, inadvertently limiting ourselves to new learnings.

As a normal person, you are vulnerable to believing information without using deep logic or having proper evidence. As long as it is seems to make sense, is accepted by a large group of people, or is spoken out by someone that you respect, you will take certain information to be fact or real. If you are asked for any evidence, you would gladly quote your sources, although unbeknownst to you, they may be highly unreliable. However, once you train your brain to think like a scientist that ceases to be the case.

Scientists are sceptics, meaning that they take time to question their beliefs. Therefore, if you present a scientist with a result or a situation, the first thing that they are likely to do is research to ensure that things are as they have been presented. Whereas a normal person would have their brain hardwired to having their beliefs come first and their explanation for the belief second, the scientific mind would have an opposite system. For example, a normal person thinking could believe that driving fast will cause a car accident, because one would lose control of the car. The belief here is that driving fast will cause an accident, whereas the explanation would be losing control of the car. The scientist would view this problem working from the end result to the belief. The first point that would be addressed is from viewing the wreckage, what caused the accident? Following which, the belief is established so as to explain what led to the accident.

When working with numbers, this would mean that even though you know an answer is correct, you need to offer evidence of its viability first and foremost. Take the car example above, the assumption of speeding causing the accident should be backed up by skid marks on the road, torn tires or any other relevant evidence. By reviewing all this evidence together, it should then be possible to paint a picture of what really happened. Therefore, you are likely to emphasize your methodology much more than your answer. In fact, in some cases you may find that you have arrived at the wrong answer, but because you used the right methodology, you are confident that you have done the right thing. Thinking like a scientist does not mean that you get it right every time. It means that you should be open to new learning.

Being skeptical applies to our own biases. Our brains are skilled at identifying the cognitive biases in other people's thinking, but may not do so when it comes to our own. This basically means that we trust our opinions deeply, and find it hard to question or justify them. Therefore if you believe the sky is blue and someone told you that it was green, you would likely object and not even bother with an explanation of your stance. However, if you were referring to a journal article on the same supposition, you are more likely to argue on that person's thinking. When thinking like a scientist, we need to be open to our own biases, so that we can question and address them to acquire more knowledge. Rather than accept our thinking as fast, firm and authoritative, thinking like a scientist demands that we can back up our opinions using reliable sources. It entails taking some time to logically arrange thoughts.

Skepticism is in essence, a reward for the scientific mind. It allows you to avoid the pitfalls of human nature so that when facing any problem, you can view it with a clear vision and eventually arrive at the truth of the matter. In addition, skepticism allows your brain to carry out a rational inquiry. This means that before you arrive at an answer, you systematically go through all the existing alternatives, eliminating those that are unnecessary and emphasizing those which are helpful. A rational inquiry means that you can see subjects from a scientific perspective, which can be particularly helpful when dealing with mathematical problems. This is because you will view a sequence or process, helping you move through the problem one step at a time. It involves making arguments based on logical steps and strategy.

Take for example, the work of an auditor. An auditor's job is to check on the books of a business, ensuring that the numbers that have been provided match with available information. The auditor usually works from the end result backwards, in an attempt to confirm or justify the result. Being skeptical and questioning irregularities is important for this position. However, to be effective, these questions need to be addressed in a logical manner, based entirely on the information provided and with no biases from previous experiences. This clarity of thought based on scientific reasoning will help the auditor arrive at a clear and reliable conclusion.

CHAPTER TWELVE:
AVOID THINKING PITFALLS

The previous chapter addresses the way that we can use skepticism to understand how our brains work to form beliefs. However, our brains can also lead us astray where we experience certain pitfalls due to our thoughts. When this happens, we as people form bad or invalid arguments in favor of our beliefs. When working with numbers, especially in finance, these thinking pitfalls can lead to you deceiving yourself rather than using your mind to propel yourself forward. There are four thinking pitfalls that can be avoided if you use scientific reasoning and these are: -

1) **Coincidences** – This is nothing more than the laws of probability in action. Probability is simply the extent to which an event is likely to occur, measured by the ratio of the favorable cases to the whole number of cases possible.

    When an event occurs, if it seems to be out of place, different from the norm or even a phenomenon it may be seen as a coincidence. The scientific mind does not accept coincidences. Instead, probability is assessed to evaluate the likelihood of the event occurring, supported by evidence or a detailed explanation.

2) **The Either/Or Phenomenon** – As human beings we like to make simple choices. This means that if presented with a range of variables, our thinking is focused on only those variables. We try to make choices based on what is presented before us. Mathematically this can be limiting and shows an inability to think outside the box. The scientific mind uses alternative reasoning. It avoids viewing the world in such a way

that you need to discredit one position and are then forced to accept the other positions. Scientists teach their brains to understand that reasoning more than either/or, that there is also the option "maybe".

3) **After the Fact Reasoning** – This basically refers to the type of superstition that attributes an outcome to a previous action. As human beings, we often have strange beliefs which we view as cause and effect. For example attributing hit marks in an examination to the fact that you used a lucky pencil. Scientists avoid this type of reasoning and have taught their brains to review things logically and systematically. This is particularly significant when analyzing numbers to get results, as any conclusion needs to be based on facts and suppositions.

4) **Tautology and Redundancy** – When starting an investigation, you may develop a hypothesis or a premise for testing. If your conclusion or claim is simply a restatement of one of the premises or hypothesis, then it is said to be redundant. Scientific thinking entails detailed investigation. It needs for the scientist to work out a reason as to the conclusion. In mathematical thinking, redundancy would be akin to starting with your formula as both the questions and the answer. It reveals minimal effort made and a lack of creativity. The brain needs to be directed towards being focused on problem solving so as to avoid redundancy.

In addition to these four thinking pitfalls are other factors that distort precepts and lead us to resist other viewpoints. This way, we become unable to open up our minds and explore the methods and benefits of scientific thinking. These are known as biases. The following are some common biases that are seen in everyday life.

Confirmation Bias

This can be defined as the tendency to interpret new evidence as confirmation of one's existing beliefs or theories. When thinking like a scientist, it is very easy to fall for this particular bias. The reason being that often times, you gather a range of variables and want them to makes sense together more than anything. This could possible make it easier for you to explain a certain result or justify some existing work. Therefore, instead of doing a thorough investigation, conclusions are accepted because they fit in with opinions. When working with numbers, the brain must think scientifically in order to avoid this bias. The reason being that different scenarios may call for different results, which can only be ascertained if a step by step strategic process is followed. As confirmation bias to some extent relies on assumption, you may receive the wrong results and experience difficulty trying to correct mistakes brought on by this bias.

Attribution Bias

This bias is defined as a cognitive bias that refers to the systematic errors made when people evaluate or try to find reasons for their own and others' behaviors. When conducting any type of research, it is imperative to carry out the study and let the results reveal themselves. When you have an attribution bias, it means that you look at a behavior or a result, and attempt to explain why it is so, without following the proper research steps to prove it. The problem here is that sometimes what is being investigated is not affected by the investigating attributes. Therefore, to think scientifically one should keep away from this bias. Instead, research should be conducted thoroughly, with all results being based on the actual findings. Mathematically, this would mean that you have worked out a problem and received an answer which may or may not be correct. However, you then go about trying to justify why the response is what it is, instead of offering a proper detailed outline of how you arrived at the answer.

Agreement Bias

Cognitive dissonance, it sounds like some kind of disease that the human brain has, and in a way, it is. We all have preferences when it comes to politics, foods, music, clothing, and anything else that we actually have a choice in, which is pretty much everything. We don't like it when our preferences are challenged or when our viewpoints are challenged, and thus we stick with websites and other people who share the same viewpoints and opinions we do in order to avoid confrontation and the questioning of our beliefs.

This bias is dangerous because it keeps up from seeing the entire issue at hand or the entire world, really. We shut ourselves off from that which makes us uncomfortable and end up missing quite a lot of interesting and relevant data.

As a real world example, let's say you're a man or a woman who will only date a potential life partner who also likes Italian food and hates sushi. You pass up on anyone who is eating out at a sushi bar or anyone who won't order spaghetti at a restaurant, which are quite a few people. You may be passing up a life partner that is ultimately very good for you because they open your horizons to new foods and adventures, and you might be very, very happy with them in the future.

So you see, sticking with only your beliefs and your preferences can be detrimental to your relationship with others.

In-group Bias

Just as we're bias toward the people we love such as family members and friends, we're negatively bias toward those we don't know, such as a stranger who moves in next door or a person who want to join a specific group. In the olden days, this may have kept up safe from a stranger trying to infiltrate our tribe and cause trouble, but now that we're a global community that needs to let go of those differences and learn to work together.

This bias actually has a lot to do with our brain chemistry, believe it or not. When we're in a group of people we know and trust, our brains release a neurotransmitter known as oxytocin, also known as the love molecule. It makes us feel good and helps us form strong bonds with those around us. Unfortunately, the same neurotransmitter also makes us feel fearful and suspicious of those who attempt to infiltrate our familiar group.

While this is helpful for everyday interactions with strangers because we don't want to become prey to a predator, we also need to understand this is happening to us when we're in business meetings or in a scientific group.

Gambler's Fallacy

It's known as a fallacy but it's actually a miscommunication in our brain. The gambler's fallacy or bias is what makes a gambler keep gambling, and often brings about the gambling addiction. For example, you've flipped a coin thirty times in a row and it's all come up with heads, so we automatically keep going because we believe that soon it has to be tails because the odds are in our favor. However, this isn't the case with statistics. The odds are still 50/50 each time the coin is flipped. The odds don't change depending upon how many times you flip the coin because it resets every time you flip that coin. Therefore, the outcome is statistically independent and the probability of the outcome is still the same.

There's also the positive expectations bias, which is highly related to the gambling addiction problem. It's the idea that eventually our luck will change, either for the better or for the good. Statistically, however, our luck remains the same each time we roll a dice or play Blackjack. It's also the same feeling we get when we begin a new relationship and believe that it will be better than the previous one. In reality, all the odds are reset every time we do something.

A scientist understands this and uses statistics in their observations. They allow themselves to not fall into the trap of gambling when they're researching a hypothesis, and they recognize when they're starting to slip.

Post-Purchase Rationalization

We've all done this and there isn't anything to be ashamed about when it comes to having this bias, but we need to recognize when we're experiencing it. If you want to think like a scientist on a daily basis, you have to not only recognize and work on avoiding scientific bias, but also the biases that make us human.

As an example, the post-purchase rationalization bias is one that affects us all when we buy something we know is a bad decision. Yet after we purchase it, we rationalize that we needed it in some way and make ourselves believe that it was a good idea all along. For instance, say you purchase a vehicle that you know you can't afford in the long-run, but you somehow obtained a loan for it. A few months later, you're still rationalizing that you needed that vehicle even though you have buyer's remorse because deep down, you know you could have bought a cheaper one.

We're subconsciously justifying our purchasing decisions.

Neglecting Probability

People have a tendency to overinflate something that is actually not that dangerous compared to underinflating their reactions to something that is *that* dangerous. For example, we tend to be more afraid of getting into an airplane than getting into a vehicle, even when we logically know that our chances of dying in a car crash are much greater than the odds of dying in a plane crash. Statistically, we're more likely to die in a vehicular accident with the odds of 1 in 84 compared to a chance of 1 in 5,000 in an airplane crash.

We're also more afraid of a terrorist attack than we are of dying from falling down the stairs or an accidental poisoning, which are both far more likely to occur than a terrorist attack.

This is known as probability neglect. We are not able to grasp a good sense of risk or peril properly and thus fear things that we shouldn't compared to things that we really ought to. This leads us to overstate a risk and the probability of becoming injured, and understate a risk that is more likely to injure or kill us.

Scientists understand and observe themselves doing this when they're investigating information. We're more likely to be afraid of the brightly colored frog than we are of the dull colored one, but in reality, the dull one might be more poisonous. That's why we investigate our theories by testing information and making our observations into truths or untruths. It's better to know for sure.

Observational Selection Bias

Have you ever noticed that when you start listening to a particular band or you start wearing a particular colored shirt, you notice more and more people wearing that that shirt or listening to that band? This is known as observational selection bias. For some reason our brains focus on things that are similar to us or focus on something because we're fascinated with it.

The truth is these things are actually not occurring at a different rate. Very rarely is that true. Our brains are just fixated on that object or phenomenon, and we seem to notice it more often. We start to believe that this isn't a coincidence, which can become very disconcerting for some.

Scientists don't automatically believe that something is happening more often just because they saw it once and their brains fixated on it. They study these occurrences and build solid proof that something is happening more often. As a scientific example, let's say scientists discover a new illness, but in reality it's actually not new. It's been around for centuries, but they just didn't have the tools to diagnose it. Now they have the tools to do so. Some of them might fall into the trap of thinking that this not so new illness is happening more often, but in reality it's just that they're able to see it now.

Status-Quo Bias

People tend to be very apprehensive about chance, and this leads to us making a choice or choices that guarantee our current status-quo stays the same or change very little. This can have very many negative effects on our daily lives as well as our long-term lives. It's often seen in politics and economics, especially in the United States government. For example, many people are in favor of the universal healthcare act; however, they're not supportive of it when they find out it means their healthcare status may change, even if it's for the better.

Scientists understand that every day things change, and they step back from a situation and view it from a logical standpoint rather than an emotional one. They might ask themselves things such as, will this make a positive or negative difference in my life or the life of someone else? Will this make a positive or negative impact on the outcome of my experiment? They don't allow their emotions to come into play.

Negativity Bias

Have you ever heard someone say that when they're passing a card accident on the highway they slow down and gawk, even though they really don't want to see anything bad? We're more apt to pay attention to bad news than we are good, but why is this? Are we morbid? Do we want to see other suffer? It's really not as bad as it might seem.

The reason we want to pay special attention to negative things happening is because we want to make sure those negative things don't affect us. For example, we turn on the news every night and look at plenty of horrible stories happening, and we're glad that we're safe and comfortable in our own homes. At least, we perceive ourselves to be safe.

While this was great for us in the past, it's not becoming detrimental to our society. Scientists argue that violence is actually declining while most of the general public would argue that it's on the rise. Why? Because they tend to pay attention to all of the negative publicity and newscasters know this, so they put up more bad stories than they do good.

Scientists understand that they cannot focus solely on the bad during an experiment. They know that there are good outcomes and that not everything is negative.

Bandwagon Effect

Most people are not conscious of the fact that they actually love to go along with the flow of a crowd. When we're at a baseball game or we're at the racetrack betting on horses, we always switch our rooting for the team that's winning or the team that everyone around us is rooting for. We start to groupthink or think in the mentality of a hive. It actually doesn't have to be a large crowd, though. Sometimes we behave this way when we're in a small group, even a family group.

The bandwagon effect or group bias is what often creates behaviors that are known as social norms, and memes to propagate amongst groups of individuals. There is no evidence or support for the way a group behaves, but they behave that way because it's acceptable. Scientists are aware of this type of thinking and they're very conscious of when they might be participating in it.

A scientist comes up with a theory of their own and only agrees with another scientist when there is evidence pointing to the both of them being correct. They sometimes slip up and will participate in groupthink, but they're aware of it when it occurs and are able to step back and think more logically.

Projection Bias

Have you ever been with someone and they agreed with every word you said, and you believed them when they agreed with you? Then you find out later they talked about the same subject with someone else and their reasons were completely against what you had both agreed on in the first place? This is known as projection bias. We oftentimes believe we're right and think that others believe us to be right without asking their opinion.

In some cases, we also believe that what is best for us is best for someone else. For example, have you ever had a relative that told you to take a certain course or path in college or life, only to find out later they had wished they'd done what they'd told you to do when they were younger? They believe that you should complete the same things they wanted to do in order for you to be a good and successful person. This happens very often with children and parents when the children are looking for a college and trying to determine what they want to do for a living.

The Current Moment Bias

When given the choice, human beings will choose pleasure for the current moment and push off experiencing pain or discomfort for later rather than just get it over with. In a study conducted in 1998, scientists discovered this phenomenon by offering the participants chocolate or fruit for that day, and had them make the decision of what they were going to eat the following week. Seventy-four percent of the participants chose to eat the chocolate that day and push off eating the fruit the following week.

How much do you want to bet they would have don't he same thing on a daily basis until that week that had been in the future was up, and they hadn't eaten fruit?

Scientists recognize when they're putting something off because they know it will cause them some sort of discomfort, whether it's emotional, mental, or physical, and they stop pushing that inevitability off to another day.

Anchoring Effect

The anchoring effect or the relativity trap is the tendency to compare and contrast a limited set of items rather than looking at the overall picture. People start to fixate on one value or number that becomes compared with everything else.

For example, say you're at a store and you see a sale item. We see the difference in price and we value that, but we don't see the overall price itself. That's why most restaurants will feature an expensive entrée and then include a more reasonably priced one, but it's actually not really reasonably priced.

So now that you recognize biases, how do you get past them?

Hindsight Bias

The final bias to watch out for is the hindsight bias, which is known as the knew it all along effect or creeping determinism, and it is the inclination, after an event has occurred, to see the event as having been predictable, despite there having been little or no objective basis for predicting it. This happens when you are working and have already got a predetermined idea of the result, so much so that when you get it you can exclaim, "You see. I knew it." The problem with the hindsight bias is once you get the results, you close your mind to further evaluation and determining whether it was possible to get some more information. A scientist never allows this to happen, as even at the end of the experiment, they do not view the end, rather they are interested in the possibilities for the future. So results are rarely viewed as predictable, and in addition, are not predicted during the testing phases.

CHAPTER THIRTEEN: SEEING THROUGH SCIENTIFIC EYES EACH DAY

This book is designed to explain how you can exercise your brain to think like a scientist every day. However, you may be surprised to note that in addition to the advice and techniques that you have read so far, you have already been exercising your brain, and are ingrained with the tools to think like a scientist.

Thinking like a scientist, or training the brain towards scientific thinking is all about methodology before you arrive at a conclusion, you will try a new way of figuring things out by looking at the situation, offering an explanation and observing its effectiveness. What makes scientific thinking different from normal thinking is the element of strategy. A strategy does not only refer to a scenario where high powered executives meet to make decisions, it also refers to the basic act of creating a plan.

As you can tell, this is simple and does not require a complex set of skills. However, when one thinks of thinking like a scientist to analyze numbers, it may seem daunting or even complex. Here are a few ways that we use science on a daily basis. By understanding them, we can teach our brains how to apply scientific thinking to more situations, especially how we deal with numbers.

The Crossword Puzzle

Completing crossword puzzles is like competing with mental acrobatics. The same methods you would use here apply to scientific problems, as well as mathematical ones. To start, you look at the clue in the puzzle and evaluate whether you understand it or not. If you understand the clue, you make a guess at the word that is meant to fit in the blanks. If you do not understand the clue or cannot figure out the answer, you skip this clue hoping that as you fill in more blanks, the solution will come to you. Scientists draw conclusions in the same way. They have trained their brains to think about clues so as to fill in the blanks in their experiments or work, and when they do not know the answer, they address other variables to draw inspiration. This is an activity that millions of people all over the world engage in on a daily basis. It encourages scientist thinking through rational, elimination and strategy.

Using a Recipe to Cook a Meal

If you have ever observed a seasoned chef at work, you will observe a combination of artistic and scientific thinking. The artistic thinking is revealed in the beauty of presentation, whereas the scientific thinking is present in the balancing of flavors.

Like a crossword puzzle, cooking begins with a guess that two ingredients will work together to produce something delicious. Once the ingredients are put together, they chef tastes the meal to see if all the ingredients have come together correctly. If it is not right, different elements are added until a balance is found. Cooking needs logical thought and many people use this reasoning on a daily basis. Mathematical problems can also have these elements, whereby if your answer is not right, you try working it out with various options until you receive the desired result.

Handling Repairs

You need to have a certain level of scientific reasoning and strategy to make repairs to your car or your plumbing for example. You start of by guessing the source of the problem. At this juncture, you need to go into the actual car or walls if it plumbing and ensure that you have been able to find the source of the problem. The reason that you are guessing is that it might sometimes not be clear. If you are able to find the source, then you can go ahead and finalize the repairs. If you have not found the source then you can begin trying out a solution (or range of solutions, eliminating those that do not work along the way) and seeing if it works. When working with numbers, you can apply these principles to get to your final answer. By narrowing down and eliminating the alternatives that do not provide answers, you can reach the right conclusion.

If you observe these examples, you will notice three main similarities that apply for scientific thinking. The first is guessing at the problem, the second is reviewing and trying the alternatives and finally checking to see if the solution worked. Working with numbers is relatively simple if you apply these principles to get you proposed output. The simplicity of teaching your brain to think scientifically is amazing. The word science need not be associated with complexity and difficulty. Perhaps being a professional scientist can be realistically viewed as difficult, but practicing scientific thinking on a daily basis is something we do easily even without realizing that we are.

CHAPTER FOURTEEN: HOW TO OVERCOME BIASES

Now that you know biases exist, you're one step closer to overcoming them both in your daily life and in your logical thinking exercises that you perform both in school and in a scientific setting.

Recognizing the Bias

The first step to overcoming a bias is knowing that one exists and that it is happening to you. Most people will readily admit biases exist, but they will not admit that they harbor a bias because admitting this means that we are in some way flawed. Just remember that all humans have biases.

Note the Three Reasons You Have a Bias

There are more than three reasons to have a bias, but these are three ones that are very common.

Strange

The object of your bias is strange to you because you don't really know anything about it and you may have heard negative things about it. You don't really know how many of those stories are true or relevant, but you believe them.

Betrayal

You may be caught up in a group bias and you feel that if you're not biased against whatever the object of your bias is, then you are betraying your group. You feel that you should be prejudiced because everyone else is, and if you're not, then you're weird or wrong.

Attractiveness

Your brain is attracted to this bias because you're not sure if you should really give it up. For example, you may be afraid and biased against those who wear trench coats because the students who committed the heinous crime of murder at Columbine wore trench coats. Therefore, for your own safety, you may feel that you should be afraid of those who wear trench coats because they might be hiding something.

Ask Questions

The third way to rid yourself of a bias is to ask questions about it. Explore the bias. You want to gain insight and lessen the grip that bias has over you. When you feel a bias rising up, ask yourself if it's fair, relevant, or worthy. Ask yourself if it really helps anyone and ask yourself how you obtained this bias. Really explore *why* you're feeling this way instead of immediately running from it.

Not only does this help you avoid biases, it helps you be a happier person when you understand why you feel a certain way and let go of those irrational fears. A bias is nothing more than being irrationally afraid of something or irrationally positive toward something. You're avoiding that bait and trap system that most people are falling into anymore.

Face It

Sometimes the best way we can over a bias is we have to face it with an open mind. This is a lot easier said than done, especially when we have an irrational fear of something. Perhaps you have a bias against a specific nationality or religion, so the best thing you can do is find a place where these people meet up on a regular basis and interact with them. Get to know the people in that room and start looking at them as people rather than as outsiders.

Look for the humanity in the people or the objects. Evaluate your feelings and ask yourself if you're really being rational about what you're thinking or feeling. Then use time to your advantage. Biases will change over time, and it takes time in order for them to change. Take everything slowly.

Take It One Step at a Time

The best thing to do with a bias is to take it one step at a time. You don't want to immerse yourself in what you perceive as wrong or even positive. Step back from it all and really think about it, mull over it. If you know you're being irrational, your bias will be that much easier to overcome.

CHAPTER FIFTEEN:
USE MODELS AND STATISTICS WISELY

When referring to someone who is a professional scientist, what often comes to mind is their focus and dedication to what they are doing. So intense is their focus that often times, scientists are referred to using the term "mad scientist". This term is supposedly to elaborate on their character and intense focus, and the assumption is that they are difficult to communicate with and understand. It is assumed that if you were to speak with them, they would use complex terms, advanced jargon and undiscernible language to explain what they are doing. Once they use these methods to communicate, the result on others is that they may switch off and the message then loses all meaning. This is a situation that applies when people are working with numbers as well. If someone were to try to communicate a mathematical problem to you using a complex formula or specialized methodology, you are unlikely to understand or connect with what is being explained.

Scientific thinking does not revolve around complicated formulas, advanced models and complex statistical methods. However, when one thinks of a scientist, this is what comes to mind. Scientists have long been viewed as geniuses, who are able to understand and explain complex situations by applying knowledge that is not found with the average person. Although there are some attributes that a scientist would have that separates them from other thinkers, the analytical and logical way that they arrive at their conclusions is something that we can all emulate and benefit from.

More often than not, scientific thinking is about following a plan or strategy to arrive at a solution. It is not about complicating a problem and its methodology to the extent that it can no longer be understood. Understanding clues and following steps is what is needed. When explaining a solution, it should be simple enough that the average person can understand the results. This is possible through employing simple diagrams and universal models and statistics to explain conclusions. Simplicity of conclusions also applies when dealing with mathematical problems. Although reaching the solution may entail use of formulas, models and statistics, explaining the methodologies in simple English is normally the right way to form the conclusion of any analysis.

In fact, complicated statistics and methodologies are used when scientists are trying to impress their peers. This is because it is often only their peers who may have any sort of understanding of these methods. Therefore, it can be assumed that use of complex methodologies is not an indication of scientific thinking or reasoning, rather it is a way to explain results and justify "knowledge".

As often happens, some people use complicated methodologies and statistics without fully understanding them or their implications. This is so that they can appear to be forward thinking, intuitive and knowledgeable. When one does not understand their methodologies or the reasons that they are being used, they may produce results that are misleading or even use methodologies that were completely unnecessary. When you are thinking like scientist, especially as you develop your mind to work with numbers, you should learn to appreciate the power of simplicity and logic, versus exaggerating processes and using complex jargon when illustrating your methodologies and conclusions.

However, it is inaccurate to say that you should not use any mathematical models or statistical methods and formulas at all. There is a reason that they are available for analyzing information. The point is to pick relatable methods, formulas or statistics. What you can opt to do is use methods that are easy to understand and interpret, to avoid your work being lost in translation, losing meaning due to wrong methodologies being used, or being rejected due to it being too difficult to understand. There are some universal methodologies that can be used when analyzing information and these include

- Frequency distributions that measure variables against each other to show you the most common occurrences. These are often expressed as a percentage for ease of understanding.

- Standard deviations which shows how measurements within a group are spread out from the average or expected value. This helps you tell how close answers are to the average and therefore how closely they are related to accepted norms.

- Correlations are used to test cause and effect relationships. They can also be used to see whether two variables are associated without having to infer a cause and effect relationship.

- Sample compositions entail being able to assess the population being tested, categorizing them and choosing a representative sample to get a good result.

Among other methods, these are easily recognizable for scientists, mathematicians and the average person. By using this, you can logically arrive at a result by thinking in a step by step fashion. In addition, using these methodologies helps you to illustrate your answers so that the people who are going through them can easily understand the point that you were trying to bring across.

When working mathematically with numbers, it is also important to be able to illustrate your answers so that they can easily be interpreted and understood.

CHAPTER SIXTEEN: THINK LIKE A MATHEMATICIAN

Thinking like a scientists and thinking like a mathematician are highly related; however, there are a few key differences in the process. You'll still need to follow the basics of thinking logically as if you were a scientist if you're focusing on numbers. In a way, mathematicians are scientists and they access the same base knowledge when they're attempting to solve a problem.

Here are the steps to thinking like a mathematician.

Question Everything

When you're attempting to solve a problem, you want to question all the data that you have in front of you. The beauty of being someone who works with solid numbers and data is that it can all be checked and you don't have to take anyone's word for it when it comes to answers. There's a process known as proving an equation, which can be very simple or complex depending on the equation in question.

The important thing to remember here is that you cannot allow people to feed you information. Your initial reaction to someone's statement should be to automatically disbelieve them until you or they prove otherwise with solid facts and reasoning. Even if the statement turns out to be true, you've mentally exercised your brain to think like a mathematician, which is the ultimate goal.

For example, a letter in a newspaper stated that time travel is not possible because logically, if it were, we would be meeting people from the future already. There are some arguments on both sides of this problem, and it all depends upon what you believe to be logically true. However, a scientists and a mathematician would take all answers into consideration and question them all, as well as their opposites to be sure those are not true.

Write in Sentences

It might seem odd for someone working with numbers to write them down in sentences, but words are the building blocks of an argument. Someone who is a true mathematician and scientists are going to look for more than just an answer, but an answer that is in the form of proof. When you write your answers down in the form of sentences, you are going to think carefully about your answer and may even find mistakes to a seemingly correct answer when you're simply using numbers.

If you're not able to write the sentence fully, then you might not have the correct answer or you might not fully understand what you're writing about. This is an excellent way to develop and expand upon your skills in both mathematics and writing.

Use Converse Statements

Mathematicians and scientists know that they need to use a statement such as A➔B. They know they need to be able to say that if A is true, then B is true. Therefore, the converse statement of A➔B is B➔A.

As an example, you might say that 'If I am George Washington, then I am American' and the converse is 'If I am American, then I am George Washington.'

The second statement is known to be impossible and untrue; therefore, the answer can be 'If I am George Washington, then I am American', but it can't be the converse. A true mathematician and scientist will explore this to sharpen and hone their skills. The question itself is not important, but the process you go through is.

Use Contrapositives

Just like the statement A➔B so B➔A, a contrapositive is A➔B and Not B➔not A. Using the same example, the answers would be 'If I am George Washington, then I am American' and the contrapositive would be 'If I am not Winston Churchill, then I am not English. Unlike a converse statement, a contrapositive statement will always be true if you have the correct answer. It's a good way to double check your work to be sure it's right.

Consider Extreme Examples

Sometimes it's best when we use an extreme example and have a stockpile of them in order to use them when we're working out a problem. Using mundane examples will trigger our minds to think in a mundane manner; therefore, instead of using a number we might use a function instead.

Create Your Own Examples

A mathematician creates their own examples, whether they're extreme or not, because they want to understand the problem inside and out. Sometimes it's easier to work with numbers we're familiar with in the beginning, and then move on to more extreme examples.

Where are Assumptions Used

The hardest part about learning proofs and being a mathematician is understanding that there are assumptions for every proof. You simply have to figure out what those assumptions are and it will help you with the problem better.

For example, Pythagoras' Theorem requires the assumption of a right angled triangle. If you don't automatically assume that in that particular proof, then everything you do is going to be for naught. You may see that some proofs refer to another proof, so be sure to check that one for assumptions, too.

Another good tip is to be sure to memorize proofs that are used often. This will help you understand proofs a lot better.

Start with the Complicated

When you're looking at a formula that's very complicated and has two sides, you want to start with the complicated side first and find any substitutions you may be able to make. For example, if you're working with an equation that looks like $A(B+6)=72$, break the equation down into $AB+A6=72$. This is a lot easier to work with when you have to take one part of the equation and add it to another.

Ask What If

When you're working with math, you're working with some assumptions. Ask yourself what would happen if you dropped those assumptions. When you ask questions about what you're doing, you're increasing your understanding and you may even discover a new loophole or an easier way to do something!

Communicate

The best thing you can do when you're trying to learn scientifically or mathematically is communicate with your peers and with your seniors. Always carry a notebook so that you can write down examples and talk with people or ask them to explain something to you. Be aware of what everyone around you is doing and ask them questions when you see them doing something you don't agree with or understand.

Collaboration is crucial between scientists and mathematicians, and it's the basic way humans learn.

Now that you know how to think like a scientist and a mathematician, get out there and start talking with your peers!

CONCLUSION

Exercising your brain to think like a scientist involves three things: the ability to pay attention to unexpected findings instead of rejecting them, methodological reasoning and the ability to look beyond a simple answer. When dealing with numbers, it is possible to train the brain towards scientific based goal orientation, whereby, one tries to explain surprising results or inferences from experiments.

Human nature means that we draw on our past experiences and existing knowledge when analyzing and explaining any results. When you choose to think like a scientist, you learn to avoid distorting results by looking for evidence that is consistent with your existing knowledge. Your focus should change to being open to unexpected findings.

Exercise your brain by changing your approach to problems. Rather than viewing problems as a barrier, view them as opportunities that open up for further discovery.

Problem solving should be your focus, rather than avoidance or frustration. If you are working on a problem, and you seem unable to find a solution, identify methods available that will allow you to further analyses the results. To think like a scientist, you should open up your mind to more experiences, and in turn explore methods to build on these experiences.

Remember that the scientist always pursue more than one solution, so evaluate your results in a way that you can get information that represents different points of view.

Exercising your brain will let you reap huge profits from having the right attitude for numbers. It is not so complicated, which you must have figured out after reading this book.

Happy Thinking!

If you enjoyed this book, kindly leave a review for this book on Amazon.

Thank you and good luck!